I Love Baby Animals

Fun Children's Picture Book with Amazing Photos of Baby Animals

By

David Chuka

www.davidchuka.com

Published By: Pen-n-a-Pad Publishing

Contact: info@davidchuka.com

Books by the Author

Billy and Monster Book Series

Billy and the Monster who Loved to Fart

Billy and Monster: The Superhero with Fart Powers

Billy and the Monster who Ate All the Easter Eggs

Billy and Monster's New Neighbor Has a Secret

Other Titles by the Author

If You See a Doctor

I Love Baby Animals

Counting to Ten and Sharing My Easter Eggs

I Love My Dog

My mom has just had a baby.

I wonder what you call baby animals in the animal kingdom?

Let's find out.

A baby lion is called a...

Cub

Lion cubs are born helpless and blind.

A baby alligator is called a...

Hatchling

A hatchling is about six to eight inches long at birth.

A baby duck is called a...

Duckling

A mother duck will lead her newly hatched ducklings to a good water source where they can swim and feed.

A baby dolphin is called a...

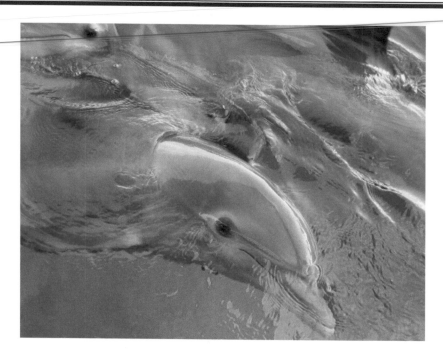

Calf

A new born calf will quickly head towards the surface of the water to get their first breath.

A baby frog is called a...

Tadpole

Tadpoles like to eat algae.

A baby dog is called a...

Puppy

A puppy will usually spend about fourteen hours every day sleeping!

A baby butterfly is called a...

Caterpillar

Caterpillars are known to eat their old skin.

A baby sheep is called a...

Lamb

Lambs can walk a few minutes after birth.

A baby turkey is called a...

Poult

A baby turkey is also called a chick.

A baby elephant is called a...

Calf

Baby elephants stay very close to their mother for the first few months of their life.

A baby hedgehog is called a...

Hoglet

A hoglet is also called a pup and they are born blind.

A baby pig is called a...

Piglet

A piglet's nose is called a snout.

A baby kangaroo is called a...

Joey

The joey will typically stay in its Mommy's pouch for about nine months.

A baby horse is called a...

Foal

A healthy foal is able to start running a few hours after birth.

A baby gorilla is called an...

Infant

An infant will usually start to walk by the time it is nine months old.

A baby llama is called a...

Cria

A cria can weigh between nine and fourteen kilograms at birth.

A baby snake is called a...

Snakelet

Snakes smell with their tongue!

A baby cat is called a...

Kitten

A kitten purring is a good sign to show it feels safe and content.

A baby eagle is called an...

Eaglet

Eaglets love to eat fish and their mommy will tear up the fish before giving them to eat.

A baby rabbit is called a...

Bunny

A baby rabbit is also called a KIT.

Do you know what a baby jellyfish is called?

THE END

Dear reader

I would like to thank you getting a copy of this book. It is always a pleasure to discover people who read my books and enjoy them. I do hope you have enjoyed reading 'I Love Baby Animals'.

If you had a nice experience reading this book with your loved one, it would really help me if you could leave a good review on Amazon. Your review might just encourage someone else to get this book for their loved one plus it also encourages me to pick up my pen and pad and write some more great stories for children!

Thank you.

David Chuka

P.S. – a baby jellyfish is called an ephyra

Questions, comments, connect?

Email - info@davidchuka.com

Blog - http://www.davidchuka.com

Sign up to my newsletter at my blog to get informed of the latest Billy and Monster Book. You also get a free Coloring and Activity Book when you sign up.

Twitter - https://twitter.com/DavidChuka

Facebook - https://www.facebook.com/Author.David.Chuka

Have You Read this Amazon Best-seller by David Chuka?

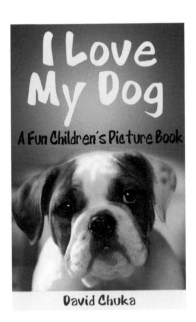

This dog book for kids was created for young children between the ages of 2 to 6. You and your loved ones will fall in love with the cute dogs in this book.

Your children will have fun discovering the names of different breeds of dogs that are accompanied with an interesting fact.

In this book, children will first of all see a certain breed of dog which is depicted in a cartoon image and then on the next page, they will discover a cute photo of that dog.

This is the second book in the series 'Animal Books for Kids.

Be sure to read Billy and Monster's Adventures at Easter time while they stayed at Grandma Chocalicious' House

Join Billy and Monster in this third episode of the series titled Billy and the Monster who Ate All the Easter Eggs.

Billy and Monster love all the holidays as they get to spend quality time together. However, their best holiday is Easter as they get to eat their favorite food...CHOCOLATE!

This year, they're spending Easter with Grandma Chocalicious who loves Chocolate even more than Billy. She's an expert at making chocolate cake, chocolate waffles and even chocolate pasta.

This year Grandma Chocalicious has made a pyramid of Easter eggs for her party on Easter Sunday. Billy and Monster want one of the Easter eggs but Grandma says they have to wait till Easter Sunday.

What happens when Billy and Monster tip toe downstairs and the pyramid of Easter eggs comes falling down?

Get your copy of this funny book for kids of all ages that is not only full of laughs but also has a lesson weaved in that you'll love sharing with your loved ones.

And the latest book from the Billy and Monster Book series

In this fourth episode in the very entertaining series for kids of all ages, Billy and Monster get to meet a new neighbor who has a secret.

Billy and Monster live on a beautiful street with some very interesting neighbors like Mr. Forgetful, Miss Squeaky and Mr. GrumpDaddy whose been banned from the local butchers. Why? Because he always gives them grief when he goes to get some beef.

On a Saturday morning while playing racing cars with Monster, they hear a knock at the door. Billy's Dad opens the door and they're introduced to their new neighbors - The FeelGoods.

After an incident involving screams and flowing streams of tears, Billy goes to Sally FeelGoods house to make peace.

And then he discovers that Sally has a COLORFUL secret that leaves Billy's mouth open as wide as the Grand Canyon.

Get your copy of this book today to discover how Billy deals with this secret in this best selling series.

I Love Baby Animals

Written by David Chuka

Text and Cartoon Image Copyright belong to David Chuka

CPSIA information can be obtained
at www.ICGtesting.com
Printed in the USA
LVHW07n0323231018
594503LV00003B/9/P